13 November 2023

To Dmitry

w/ ♡ and prayers...

Staynt...

♪

fortuna flow

poetry

volume i

fr stan fortuna cfr

Copyright © 2021 by fr. stan fortuna
Published by Francesco Productions
420 East 156th Street
The Bronx, New York 10455
www.francescoproductions.com
First Edition October 2022

ISBN: 979-8-218-06486-0

Library of Congress Control Number: 2022919476

Printed in the United States of America

Front Cover Photography
by David Gonzalez

for additional copies

call:

718.401.1589

write:

fortuna flow

poetry volume i

420 East 156th Street

The Bronx, New York 10455

email:

flowfortuna9@gmail.com

francescoproductions

www.francescoproductions.com

frstan@francescoproductions.com

fortuna flow

poetry

volume i

table of contents

introduction

Fr. Stan Fortuna, CFR

Stan Fortuna was born on June 9, 1957, in Yonkers, New York. He joined the Capuchin Franciscans in 1979. In 1987, along with seven other Capuchin friars under the leadership of Fr. Benedict Groeschel, he helped with the founding of a new community - The Franciscan Friars of the Renewal in the South Bronx, New York City.

Ordained a priest of Jesus Christ on December 8, 1990, Fr. Stan's commitment to the community's life of working with the poor and evangelization increased tremendously. Having left behind a life in the world of music, the Spirit of the Lord and the art of improvising intermingled, resulting in a whirlwind of renewal in the realm of music with melodies, notes, and words. Having studied with the great Lennie Tristano - one of the greatest jazz improvisers of the 20th century – Fr. Stan was equipped to build upon the disciplined foundation of the spontaneous world of improvisation, taking on the challenge for a new evangelization by the great John Paul II.

Compositions, hymns, lyrics, and books soon flowed from his rich and diverse experiences – many of which have contributed to this current first volume of his poetry. Proceeds from the sales of his recordings and books assist in the community's work with the poor through his nonprofit Francesco Productions. Participating in the community's work of preaching as an "itinerant preacher," Fr. Stan was sent nationally and internationally to preach, sing, and improvise. Those he met in the streets of New York, Toronto, Brazil, Krakow, Rome, and Assisi, as well as countless other places around the globe - in Europe, Asia, India, Africa, South America, Australia, and New Zealand – contributed to his crossing "the unbridgeable gap" described by John Paul II in his 1999 *Letter to Artists (#6)*:

All artists experience the unbridgeable gap which lies between the work of their hands, however successful it may be, and the dazzling perfection of beauty glimpsed in the ardor of the creative moment: what they manage to

experience in their…creating is no more than a glimmer
of the splendor which flared for a moment before the eyes
of their spirit.

Fr. Stan's spiritual father Francesco d'Assisi was a poet as was his major hero, Saint Pope John Paul II the Great. The following from John Paul II to the Pontifical Council for Culture (March 18, 1994) regarding the influence of the saints is as inspiring as it is prophetic:

The influence of the saints is decisive: through the light
that they emanate, through their inner freedom, through
the power of their personality, they have made a mark on
the artistic thought and expression of entire periods of our
history. It is enough to mention St. Francis of Assisi. He
had a poet's temperament, something which is amply
confirmed by his words, his attitude, and his innate sense
of symbolic gesture. Although his concerns were far
removed from the world of literature, he was, nevertheless,

the creator of a new culture, both in thought and in art. A St. Bonaventure or a Giotto could not have developed had it not been for him. This, dear friends, is where the true requirements of Christian culture dwell. This marvelous creation of man can flow only from contemplating the mystery of Christ and from listening to his word, put into practice with total sincerity and unreserved commitment, following the example of the Virgin Mary. Faith frees thought and opens new horizons to the language of poetry and literature, to philosophy, to theology, and to other forms of creativity proper to the human genius. You are called to develop and to promote this culture…in this world which is seeking beauty and truth, unity and love.

"Saint Francis of Assisi had a poet's temperament, something which is amply confirmed by his words, his attitude, and his innate sense of symbolic gesture. Although his concerns were far removed from the world of literature, he was, nevertheless, the creator of a new culture, both in thought and in art."

Pope Saint John Paul II
March 18, 1994

MM 33 LINES

December 21, 2014

MOTHER MARY

MYSTERIOUS MADNESS

BOUNDLESS GLADNESS

BOUND TO EARTH

BETHLEHEM'S BIRTH

BAMBINO'S WORTH

BREAD BROKEN

WORD SPOKEN

FLESH TAKEN

LOVE AWAKENED

LIFE AND LIGHT

SILENT NIGHT

DARKNESS MADE BRIGHT

HUMILITY'S MIGHT

INCARNATION

LIBERATION

NEW CREATION

THE VOCATION

FOR EVERYONE

YOUR FIRSTBORN SON

FOREVER BEGUN

NEVER TO END

PEACE TO EXTEND

FOR ENEMY AND FRIEND

EVERY COLOR

UNIVERSAL MOTHER

OF CHILDREN FAR

OF CHILDREN NEAR

TRANSFORMING FEAR

ETERNITY CLEAR

ALREADY HERE

CELESTIAL MATERNITY

AVE MARIA MOTHER MARY

FOOD OVER HERE

Rome ~ November 3, 2014

MAKE ME BE

READIED WITH DIGNITY

LIKE FOOD OVER HERE

SERVED WITHOUT FEAR

SALTED WITH AMAZEMENT

EVERY ENCOUNTER INCREASING

LOVE'S QUALITY EXPANDING

LOVE'S EVER MORE DEMANDING MORE

FOR GREATER PLEASURE IN GIVING

CONSUMPTION OF LOVE

DIGESTED IN MY 'BEING'

BEING POURED OUT

IN MY DYING ~ IN MY LIVING

LOVING ETERNITY NOW ~ HERE

FEEDING ON LOVE

THAT'S NOT SYMBIOTIC BUT

RATHER REALIZED UNION

FRUITFUL COMMUNION

WITH NO DOCTRINE TO CHANGE

MADE MAGNANIMOUS BY LOVE

WITH ME REARRANGED

NARROWNESS OF HEARTS EXCHANGED

FOR UNIMAGINABLE HEIGHTS

LIBERATED BY INCONCEIVABLE

BURNING LIGHTS

FRACTIONING DETAILS

OF ALL ORTHODOX

EUCHARISTIC RITES SO THAT

AS THE CHURCH BITES

THE WORLD MIGHT

TASTE DELIGHTS

OF LOVE

MAKING ME MORE

LIKE FOOD

OVER HERE

YOUR FIRST VIGIL FEAST

Krakow ~ October 21, 2014

WHAT DID YOU THINK

HOW DID YOU PRAY

WHAT DID YOU SAY

TO LET YOURSELF GO

THAT KAROL WOJTYLA WAY

WONDERING AS I SIT

ON THE EVENING VIGIL

OF YOUR FIRST FEAST

FROM THAT SAME SEAT

ON FRANCISZKANSKA STREET

WHERE YOU FREQUENTLY SAT

AND STILL MYSTERIOUSLY SIT

I ADMIT

I'D LIKE TO PERMIT

LOVE TO EXPLAIN

EVERYTHING TO ME

PLEASE PRAY THIS LOVE

MAY MAKE ME READY

AND FIND ME READY

TO BE SET FREE

AL-LE-LU-IA

JEN-KU-IA

ROMAN MARKET

Rome ~ November 4, 2006

GOT THEIR HANDS

ALL OVER THE FOOD

LOVE THE FOOD

WITH LOVE

LOVE IS THE FOOD

LOVE TO EAT

EAT TO LOVE

EAT THE LOVE

TOUCH WITH LOVE

THE FOOD OF LOVE

LOVE TO WORK

THE WORK OF LOVE

TO LOVE SO MUCH

AS TO COMMIT

AND PERMIT

ONESELF

TO BE EATEN

"Farmers everywhere provide bread for all humanity, but it is Christ alone who is the bread of life. He alone satisfies the deepest hunger of humanity. As Saint Augustine said: 'Our hearts are restless until they rest in you (Confessions I, 1).' While we are mindful of the physical hunger of millions of our brothers and sisters on all continents, at this Eucharist we are reminded that the deepest hunger lies in the human soul. To all who acknowledge this hunger within them, Jesus says: 'Come to me all you who are weary and find life burdensome, and I will refresh you.' My brothers and sisters in Christ: Let us listen to these words with all our heart. They are directed to every one of us. To all who till the soil, to all who benefit from the fruit of their labors, to every man and woman on earth, Jesus says: 'Come to me…and I will refresh you.' Even if all the physical hunger of the world were satisfied, even if everyone who is hungry were fed by his or her own labor or by the generosity of others, the deepest hunger of man would still exist."

John Paul II October 4, 1979
Des Moines Iowa – Living History Farms

19

FRINGE MASTER

en route to fr. benedict's burial day

October 10, 2014

FRINGE MASTER

JERSEY CITY BLASTER

MEDICINE FOR THE DISASTER

HEALING WOUNDS OF NON-LOVE

FEELING "THE CONFESSIONS"

DEEP DOWN IN MEMORY

GROESCHEL

FAITHFUL SON OF GETHSEMANE

REFORMING PATHS AHEAD OF ME

PSYCHOLOGY'S ANATOMY

MAKING MORE REAL SPIRITUALITY

AS LOVE POURED OUT

WITH FREEDOM SERVING THE POOR

FOOD SHELTER AND CLOTHING

GIVEN WITH LOVE FOR SURE

YOUR LEGACY WILL ENDURE

ONLY TO THE DEGREE THAT WE

TRUST PROVIDENCE TO LEAD

LIKE YOU - WILLINGLY

TO LET OUR SOULS BLEED

WITH BLOOD OF A REFORMED FLOOD

OF LOVE FOR WHICH WE ASK YOU

NOW TO INTERCEDE

OUR DEAR FATHER BENEDICT

HELP US LOVE THE HERETIC

HELP US LOVE THE DERELICT

WITH THAT RADICAL LOVE

EVER ANCIENT AND EVER NEW

THIS LOVE

FRANCISCAN FRIARS OF THE RENEWAL

MUST BE AND DO

MORE AND MORE LIKE YOU

OUR BROTHER AND FATHER

FRINGE MASTER

JERSEY CITY BLASTER

MEDICINE FOR THE DISASTER

HEALING EVERY WOUND

OF NON-LOVE

"God has given me the grace to see that at the very heart of all reality burns an unquenchable love that can heal even the worst pains and sadnesses of life."

Fr. Benedict

AT YOUR FUNERAL

Newark, New Jersey – October 10, 2014

O GOD WHO IS LOVE

DECOMPARTMENTALIZE MY HEART

ALL MY HEART - EVERY PART

LIKE GRAIN INTO THE GROUND TO DIE

CANONIZE THE LOVE YOU ARE

THE LOVE I GIVE - NO LONGER I

TO LIVE TO REALIZE

THE RE-SIZE OF TRANSFORMATION

THE CORE OF POST-GROESCHELIAN

CFR ON-GOING REFORMATION

BIRTHING THE GLORIOUS FREEDOM

OF LOVE'S GLORY TAKING UP

YET AGAIN THE STORY TOLD

ALWAYS NEW NEVER OLD

BY CHILDREN OF MOTHER CHURCH

FEARLESS WITH INDEFATIGABLE ZEAL

RENDERED RESTED IN THE

RESTLESS SEARCH TO FEEL

THE FINDING OF THE NEXT GOOD STEP

TO BE TAKEN

OH GOD WHO IS LOVE

AWAKEN MY SOUL WITH LYRE AND HARP

FOR ME TO SING - TO BRING

THE LIGHT OF LOVE

AWAKENING THE DAWN

RENEWING ALL SINGERS

OF THE NEW SONG

IN WEAKNESS MADE STRONG

WITH PERFECT LOVE

PERFECTING US ALL ALONG THE WAY

STARTING AFRESH FROM TODAY

BENNIE ON YOUR FUNERAL DAY

AS WE PRAY FOR YOU

PLEASE PRAY FOR US…

VETERANS DAY 2014

The Bronx ~ November 11, 2014

SILENT CRIES

SILENT SCREAMS

INCARNATING DARKNESS

LIVING STREAMS

MEMORIES OF DEATH

LEGIONS OF SOULS

LOSING THEIR BREATH

BREATHING NO LONGER

YET NOW MORE ALIVE

MYSTERIOUSLY STRONGER

WHILE EVIL SUSTAINS

NEW WARS NEW CASUALTIES

NEW UNDETECTABLE CIRCUMSTANCES

CARRYING THE SAME PAINS

SOLDIERS HEROISM CONQUERING

STILL THE SAME BEAST

VETERANS WAR MEMORIALS

CELEBRATING THE *I WISH*

WE DIDN'T HAVE TO HAVE IT FEAST

YES, TO SAY NOT THE LEAST

WORLD WAR II IS OVER

WHILE WOUNDS OF NON-LOVE

CONTINUE TO INCREASE

THE COMBAT TAKES ON

MORE DEVASTATING PROPORTIONS

ON VETERANS DAY

REMEMBERING AGAIN

OUR BELOVED DECEASED

PASCHAL DYNAMIC

Munich ~ March 27, 2016

Easter Sunday

DARKNESS OF NIGHT

VICTORIOUS LIGHT

EXPLOSION OF SIGHT

VISION TO SEE

IN THE VISIBLE

THE INVISIBLE

PASCHAL DYNAMIC

CALMING COSMIC PANIC

LOVE'S FIRE AND FLAME

SOOTHING INCONSOLABLE PAIN

RAINING DOWN MERCY

TO BEGIN AND SUSTAIN

VISION OF PROPHET BARUCH

WISDOM'S FOUNTAIN AND BROOK

FLOWING THROUGH FOUNDATIONS

SHAKEN ONLY TO AWAKEN

LOVE THAT GROWS WHEN TAKEN

BY NO ONE BUT RATHER

IS FREELY GIVEN

MERCY'S MYSTERY NOW READY

FOR ALL TO BE LIVIN

IN THE HEART OF THE WORLD

DURING PASCHAL TIME

SATURATING ORDINARY TIME

MORE AND MORE OF THE TIME

DAY TIME ~ NIGHT TIME

ALL THE TIME

TILL THE END OF TIME

CRY FOR HELP

Masaka Uganda ~ August 18, 2008

I CAN HEAR THEIR CRY FOR HELP

AS I BEHOLD THEIR FACES AND SEE

THE WEIGHT OF BEING IN NEED

INVISIBLE PIERCING OF HEARTS

THAT BLOODLESSLY BLEED

WAITING FOR

THE CHALLENGE OF FREEDOM

TO RESCUE SOMEONE'S NEPHEW

ANOTHER'S NIECE

BOTH PART OF A PIECE

OF THE CROSS

SOMEONE'S SON OR DAUGHTER

PLUNGED INTO THE DEPTH OF TEARS

TORRENTIALLY FLOWING

NOT WITH WATER

BUT RATHER ON THE LEVEL OF BEING

WHICH ILLUMINES MY SEEING

FROM WITHIN MY HEART FEELING

THE ONGOING ORIGINAL PAIN OF SIN

NO MATTER THE PLANETARY LOCATION

OF TOWN OR VILLAGE

THESE ARE MY NEXT-A-KIN

COMMUNITY A POSSIBILITY?

WHY AIN'T THIS CRY

CLOSER TO YOU AND ME?

RESPONSIBILITY OF HUMANITY

TO REVERSE THE CURSE? WHAT'S WORSE?

LIVING IN DENIAL OR TAKING A WHILE

TO BECOME LIKE A CHILD

SO THE KINGDOM I COULD ENTER

ROOTED AND GROUNDED IN THE CENTER

OF LOVE'S MYSTERY

BECOMING CHARITABLY WILD

GLOBAL DESTINY

FOR EVERYONE TO GET

THE VERY BEST OF ME

THE MOVEMENT ON EARTH

OF HEAVEN'S SYMPHONY

COMMUNION OF PERSONS

THAT'S PART OF ME

REALITY OF DIVINE LOVE'S HARMONY

CAN YOU HEAR THE CRY FOR HELP?

WILL YOU LISTEN?

GIVE PERMISSION

FOR YOUR HEART'S

SUBMERSIVE SUBMISSION

TO THE SOLUTION OF LOVE'S REVOLUTION

TO HEAL THE FEAR

TO HEAR THE CRY

FOR HELP

POURING OUT LOVE

Assisi ~ November 2, 2011

WINDOW OF ETERNITY

BIRTHING NEW HUMANITY

LOVE'S FULL MATERNITY

IN FRONT OF YOUR ICON

WITH FAITH IN SUCH LOVE

THROUGH HUMAN ART FORM

TO INFORM ~ PLEASE NOW REFORM

WITH THE BODY OF YOUR FIRSTBORN

HIS FLESH TORN ~ YOUR HEART PIERCED

THROBBING WITH THE SAME PAIN

YOURS THE SWORD ~ HIS THE NAILS

ONLY TRUTH AND LOVE

CAN REMOVE THE SCALES

COVERING EYES SO VISION

BECOMES CLEAR ~ CLEAN

WITH PERFECT LOVE

CASTING OUT FEAR

FOR MEMORIES TO HEAL

TO FEEL HEART AND SOUL

BURSTING INTO FLAME

ETERNITY DOES SOMETHING SO GOOD

WITH TIME'S DAILY PAIN

IN FRONT OF YOUR ICON

MOTHER MARY MOTHER OF ZION

MOTHER OF STUPENDOUS LOVE

WITH WHICH GIOTTO PAINTED HIS FRESCOS

ALL OVER THE BASILICA

THAT'S FRANCESCO'S

HERE AGAIN IN ASSISI

ONE MORE COUNTLESS TIME

OVER AND OVER

TILL TIME IS ALL OVER

AND WE PASS THROUGH THIS WINDOW

INTO WHICH I LOOK AT YOUR ICON

AND SEE YOU

POURING OUT LOVE

SHE WAS STANDIN

Mbarara, Uganda ~ January 9, 2011

The Baptism of The Lord

SHE WAS STANDIN

LEANIN

ON A PIECE OF WOOD

IF SHE COULD STAND

WITH POWER OF HER OWN BONE

WOULD IT CHANGE HER POWER

TO WITHSTAND THE TONE

OF A BODY BROKEN?

EVERY HEALTHY ONE

IS ONLY ON LOAN

GIFT RECEIVED

EVEN FOR MINDS THAT

HAVE NEITHER KNOWN

OR BELIEVED

MYSTERY'S EVIDENCE

SOUL'S TAKIN RESIDENCE

IN SHELLS OF FLESH

SHE WAS STANDIN

LEANIN ON LOVE POURED OUT

GIVING HER BEST

HER PAIN

YOU COULD CUT IT

SLICE IT WITH A KNIFE

WHAT ARE WE DOIN

WITH THIS THING CALLED LIFE?

WHAT'S THE PURPOSE

OF FUNCTION FRENZIED PRODUCTION

WHILE OUR DEEPEST NEED

IS IN NEED OF RECONSTRUCTION?

COULD IT BE WE ARE HOPELESS?

WE WILL BE

UNLESS WE TAKE NOTICE

OF LOVE…

LOVE STANDIN

LEANIN

ON A PIECE OF WOOD

MORE THAN THESE

The Bronx ~ April 10, 2016

The 3rd Sunday of Easter

MORE THAN THESE

PLEASE LOVE ME MORE

SO THE DOOR CAN OPEN WIDE

NO LONGER I TO HIDE FROM THEE

THE CAPACITY IN ME TO SEE ME

BE MORE LIKE YOU

IN LIEU OF ALL WHO RENDEZVOUS

EXPANDING WITH THE MORE OF LOVE

FOR THE ALL OF LOVE

MERCY'S DESCENDING

INTO THE MAELSTROM

OF HUMAN MISERY

REACHING DEEP DOWN

RESTORING HUMAN DIGNITY

TO RESCUE ALL INCLUDING ME

WITH REDEMPTION SECURE

IN THE PROTECTION

OF THE ONGOING PERFECTION

OF LOVE MOVING

THE SUBJECTION OF MY WILL

TO GREATER HEIGHTS BURNING

BURNING WITH THE FIRE OF

GETTING-LOVE-DONE LEARNING

WITH GREATER LIGHTS ON EARTH

AS IT IS IN HEAVEN

SOOTHED BY THE BEATIFIC BREEZE

PLEASE HELP THE REMAINING TIME

OF MY NIGHTS AND DAYS

TO MAKE ME LOVE YOU MORE

MORE THAN THESE

173 WORDS IN SOLITUDE

Crestone, Colorado ~ December 31, 2013

MOUNTAINS

PLACED AS FOUNTAINS

FOR REVELATION

TO FLOW AND DESCEND

FOR LOVE TO EXTEND

THE MORE

FOR ALL WHO THIRST

TO COME AND DRINK

TO THINK

WITH LOVE GIVEN

FOR OUR LIVIN

WHEN WE SINK DEEP

IN DESPAIR'S DELUSION

TO LIBERATE LOVE FROM

ALL LOVE-LESS ILLUSION

LOOK WHAT TOOK PLACE

THE MYSTERY PRESENT ALREADY

ON EVERY HUMAN FACE

FOR SHAME'S DISGRACE

TO PRESS ITS LIPS

TO THE FOUNTAIN

TO DRINK AND TASTE

THE SOURCE OF EVERY LOCATION

THE FORCE OF EVERY VOCATION

FLOWING INTO SOLITARY

ABSORBING ALL FORMS OF

CULTURAL INTERNATIONAL HATING

DISSIPATING HESITATING HEARTS

RELUCTANT TO PLUNGE WILLINGLY

INTO LOVE'S VOLCANIC ABYSS

WHICH ALONE RENDERS US READY

TIME AND TIME AGAIN

TO COMMENCE THE SCATHING ASCENT

FULFILLING LOVE'S DIVINE WILL

PERFECTING LOVE'S UNIVERSAL SKILL

BOUNCING BACK FROM EVERY FALL

FROM EVERY ATTACK

WITH *LOVE YOUR ENEMIES* LOVE

HIGH ON THE PEAKS INEBRIATED

WITH THE PEACE OF FORGIVENESS

SINGING THE SONG

OF THE DOVE FROM ABOVE

LOVE BENDS DOWN

OVER THE MOUNTAINS

FROM WHENCE COMES

OUR HELP

NEW SAINTS

Munich ~ March 20, 2016

Palm Sunday

SAINTS COME

SAINTS GO

LIVING TO TELL

WHAT WE MUST KNOW

LOVE WE MUST SHOW

SUCH THUS MUST FLOW

IN HEAVEN

AND NOW BELOW

TORRENTIALLY POURING OUT

LOVE'S LIQUID FIRE

PROVIDENTIALLY SUSTAINING

LOVE'S HOLY DESIRE

TO PROLIFICALLY INSPIRE

NEW SAINTS TO COME

NEW SAINTS TO GO

LIVING TO TELL

WHAT WE MUST KNOW

LOVE WE MUST SHOW

SUCH THUS MUST FLOW

NOW AND FOREVER

INSTITUTION

The Bronx ~ May 29, 2016

Corpus Christi

INSTITUTION

AS A NOUN

IS PROFOUND

BECAUSE JESUS FOUND

THE CHURCH

INSTITUTION

"TO INSTITUTE"

A VERB

WILL DISTURB

THE STRUCTURE

INCITE A RUPTURE

SO WE DON'T HOLD BACK

SO WE YEARN

THAT WE BURN WITH CHARITY

ENLIVENED BY COMMUNION

FREE FOR LOVE'S POSSIBILITY

SPAWNING UNIVERSAL TRANQUILITY

REDEEMING ECCLESIAL STERILITY

STREAMING EUCHARISTIC CREDIBILITY

SUSPENDING PRIDE WITH HUMILITY

THE EXTREMITY OF THE MYSTERY

CHRIST LIVING IN ME

THE CALL FOR US ALL

THE REVOLUTION

THE SOLUTION

INSTITUTION

LOVE'S PERFECTION

The Bronx ~ March 18, 2008

THE CROWN OF THORNS

ADORNS CALLS AND WARNS

EMPTINESS TO FILL

WITH LOVE THAT EMBRACES

ALL THE FACES OF TRAGIC CASES

WHERE PEOPLE FEEL UNWANTED

THE GREATEST POVERTY

ENRICHES YOU AND ME

PROOFS GIVEN FROM ETERNITY

NOW ~ HERE TO CLEAR AWAY FEAR

TO BE DRAWN NEAR

LOVE'S PERFECTION

INCREASING PROTECTION

FROM DARK INTROSPECTION

INJECTING LUMINOUS INFECTION

IGNITING FIRE FOR DESIRE

TO INSPIRE POWER

PERFECTED IN WEAKNESS

THE EXTREME HUMILITY

OF MEEKNESS

TO RIDE THE HORSE OF MY PRIDE

CRUSH IT AND MAKE ME

THIRSTY FOR MERCY

FLOWING WITH

TORRENTIAL RIVERS

MAKING GENEROUS GIVERS

WITH NUCLEAR FISSION

OF LOVE EXPLODING

GIVES ME THE SHIVERS

MAKES ME SHAKE

LIKE A HUMAN EARTHQUAKE

THIS KIND OF LOVE

IS HARD TO TAKE

CAUSE IT MAKES ME BE

WHO I AM MEANT TO BE

FREE…

TO DO WHAT

I AM DESTINED TO DO

BREAKTHROUGH…

ATTEND TO THE LOVE

FLOWING FROM

THE CROWN OF THORNS

THAT ADORNS CALLS AND WARNS

EMPTINESS TO FILL

WITH LOVE WHICH EMBRACES

ALL THE FACES

OF TRAGIC CASES

WHERE PEOPLE FEEL UNWANTED

THE GREATEST POVERTY

ENRICHES YOU AND ME

ETERNALLY

NOW

HERE TO CLEAR AWAY FEAR

TO BE DRAWN NEAR

LOVE'S PERFECTION

FOREVER

ALL SAINTS

Rome ~ November 1, 2015

ALL SAINTS

GREAT TRIBULATION

GREAT DISTRESS

YET LOVE

IMPULSES BLESS

MOMENTS LIKE BREAD

MADE FRESH

WARM

EVEN HOT

THERE'S NOT A LOT

JUST A FEW

SOME DAMPENED

BY SELF-INFLICTED DEW

YET DAILY NEW

THE MORNING DEW

TO RENEW

IN THE FLESH

WE CHEW

NO LONGER I

NOW YOU

TO DO ON EARTH

SHATTERED BY BIRTH

BIRTH THAT'S DEATHLESS

WE BECOME BREATHLESS

NO MORE BREATH

NO MORE TRIBULATION

ONLY ONE SITUATION

LOVE'S NEW CREATION

ENDLESS CELEBRATION

LOVE'S VOCATION

WITH PERFECT TRANSLATION

IN ALL THE SAINTS

"The Saints …drank from the fountain of Christ's love to the point that they were transformed and in turn became overflowing springs to quench the thirst of the many brothers and sisters they met on life's path."

John Paul II March 7, 1999 Beatification
Ana Schafer, Nicolas Barré, Vicente Soler
and his six Augustinian Recollect companions

THE LAST TIME?

The Bronx ~ May 13, 2012

Mother's Day

IS THE LAST TIME

THE LAST TIME?

OR WAS THE LAST TIME I SAW YOU

LINKED FOREVER TO THE FIRST TIME

I WAS ABLE TO SEE AND SAW YOU

LOOKING AT ME WITH LOVE

MOTHER OF MY EXISTENCE

TAKEN AWAY AS YOU DART ABOUT

LIKE A SPARK THROUGH STUBBLE

ILLUMINATING WITH SOOTHING LIGHT

THE MARK OF PAIN'S TROUBLE

INDELIBLY MARKED ON MY SOUL

AND ALL OF ME

HISTORICALLY PASSING

WITH THIS MYSTERIOUS PERSISTENCE

THAT RELENTLESSLY HAUNTS ME

AND EVERYONE WHO LOSES THIS LOVE

OR WHO NEVER KNEW THIS LOVE TO LOSE

IN THE FIRST PLACE

THIS GIFT OF MOTHER LOVE

STILL ALWAYS REMAINING

IN MY HEART AWAKENED

AS YOU WERE TAKEN FROM ME

NOT HAVING YOU HERE

AS YOU USED TO BE

TO DO WHAT YOU USED TO DO

IN THE WAY ONLY YOU COULD DO

AND YET NOW EVER MORE CLOSER TO ME

EXPANDING THE BOND OF *BEING*

BEING INSEPARABLY CONNECTED TO ME

THE SAME YOU WHO BIRTHED ME

THROUGH THE LAST TIME I SAW YOU

WITH EVERLASTING COMMUNION

BRINGING INTO LOVE'S UNION

ALL THOSE DAYS TILL NOW

ALWAYS SOMEHOW

STILL TO BE TO ME MOTHER

WITH THE LAST TIME

LINKED WITH THE FIRST TIME

FULFILLING TIME

TILL THE END OF TIME

WITH THE REMAINING TIME

FOR ME TO BE MORE

LIKE YOU

TO DO MY BEST

TO BE MY BEST

TO GIVE MY BEST

TILL MY LAST BREATH

FOR ALL THE REST

OF MY DAYS

WITH LOVE

GRIEVING YOUR LOSS

The Bronx ~ 2009

GRIEVING YOUR LOSS

IS LIKE TRAVERSING A COURSE

THROUGH MOUNTAINS

MAKES MY TEARS FLOW

LIKE FOUNTAINS

FOR MANY NOW TO COME AND DRINK

IT HAPPENS TO ME

EVERY TIME OF YOU I THINK

TEARS BECOME LIKE LAKES

UNFATHOMABLY DEEP

RISING UP AND SUBMERGING

THE HIGHEST PEAK

TAKING ME HIGH AND LOW

UP AND DOWN MOVEMENTS PROFOUND

THROUGH SKY AND GROUND

WITH ROOTS DEEP AND BOOTS TIED TIGHT

STREAMS OF LIGHT PIERCING THE DARK

CUTTING THROUGH

THE CROSS TREE'S BARK

I'M MISSING YOUR WARM SHOCK

THAT ALWAYS IGNITES A SPARK

MAKIN ME BURN READY TO TAKE MY TURN

REMEMBERING THE LOVE TO LEARN

THAT YOU DID DAILY LIVE

BY WHICH YOU STILL TEACH ME

DEATH TOOK YOU AWAY AND YET

YOU STILL REACH ME

READY ALWAYS TO GIVE

GENEROUSLY

YES NOT PERFECTLY

BUT IN A WAY THAT NOW CARRIES ME

THE HEART OF YOUR LEGACY

IMMEDIATELY PERCEPTIBLE

FOR ALL TO SEE

FRUITS NOW BLOSSOMING

IN MEMORY OF YOU

NOW LIVING IN ME

CONNIE

MY MOMMY

WE LOVE YOU

FASCINATE

The Bronx ~ April 2012

I SEE THEM IT'S YOU

IT'S NOT YOU IT'S ME

IT'S NOT ME IT'S WE

SO RADICALLY FREE

ART THOU

MY SOUL BOWS DOWN

EVEN AS I WALK

SILENCE WHILE PEOPLE TALK

HUMANS WITH VISION

LIKE A HAWK

EAGLE EYE

I WON'T EVEN TRY TO FLY

TO COMPREHEND

HOW YOU CALL YOURSELF

FRIEND LOVING WITH LOVE

STRONGER THAN DEATH

TO THE END

WITH YOUR HEART YOU BEND

RIGHT DEEP DOWN INTO MY MISERY

GIVING ME FAITH TO SEE

IN THE DARK

WITH LOVE'S LIGHT

EVERYTHING WILL BE ALL RIGHT

CAUSE ETERNITY IS

NOT FAR AWAY FROM ME

NOR FAR AWAY FROM ALL

THE NEXT LIFE

IS NOT FAR AWAY AT ALL

CAUSE IT'S YOU

IT'S NOT A PLACE

IT'S THE LIGHT OF LOVE

69

SHINING FROM YOUR FACE

MELTING ALL HESITATION

CARRYING ME ALONG

WITH FASCINATION

AS YOU FASCINATE ME

WITH YOU

ADVENTUS

(ARRIVAL)

The Bronx ~ December 8, 2018

CAPTURE THE RAPTURE

BREACH THE BROKEN

SILENT WORD SPOKEN

MASSES PAIN SWOLLEN

HEARTS SHATTERED IGNORED

YET DIGNITY RESTORED

A CHILD ADORED

THE MOTHER STORED

ALL THESE THINGS

IN HASTE SHE SINGS

THE MYSTERIOUS SONG

THE 144K LEARNS

CANTORING FIRE THAT BURNS

DRAWING WAYWARD SOULS

TO RETURN TO RELEARN

LOVE AND CONCERN ALONE

WHICH FURNISH FATHER'S HOUSE

THE ONE WITH MANY ROOMS

WHOSE COMING PRESENCE LOOMS

SHROUDED IN MYSTERY

ACCELERATING HISTORY

TO ITS MOMENTOUS TRANSITUS

THE TREMENDOUS ADVENTUS

LAKE ONTARIO GLASS

Toronto ~ September 9, 2016

ONTARIO

LAKE DESIGNATED GREAT

SPEWING FORTH GLASS

CHARGED WITH UNEXPECTED BEAUTY

ONTARIO

AWESOME LAKE

DESIGNATED GREAT

DRAWING ME IN TO PARTICIPATE

YOU DEVASTATE

PIERCING MY SOUL'S EYE TO LOOK

THROUGH THE LIQUID PAGES

OF YOUR INDESCRIBABLE BOOK

FLOWING WITH TRANQUILITY

RELINQUISHING MY PRIDE

WITH YOUR HUMILITY

REVEALING THE STRENGTH

CONTAINED IN OUR FRAGILITY

LENDING CREDIBILITY

TO THE POSSIBILITY

OF MY BROKEN PIECES

BECOMING BEAUTIFUL TOO

IT'S SO MUCH LESS

MY SEEKING AND FINDING

THE WAY YOU BLESS

OVERWHELMINGLY REMINDING

BLINDING MY WAITING

WITH BRILLIANCE

PROVIDING GLASS TRANSFORMED

WITH RESILIENCE

CONTENDING WITH HISTORY'S

DISREGARD AND REJECTION

NOW FIRING MYSTERIES

OF BEAUTY AND PROTECTION

RENEWING MY LOOKING

AGAIN AND AGAIN AT YOUR GLASS

ACCUMULATING A COLLECTION

SUSTAINING UNCEASING RECOLLECTION

SPAWNING COURAGEOUS LOVE

FOR LOVE'S ONGOING PERFECTION

REGARDLESS OF THE SELECTION

OF YOUR MYRIAD BROKEN PIECES

ONTARIO

LAKE DESIGNATED GREAT

GREAT IS THE LOVE

JUST ONE PIECE

BROKEN CAN RELEASE

GREAT IS THE LOVE UNSPOKEN THEREIN

THAT LOVE CAN MYSTERIOUSLY INCREASE

FOR EACH PASSERBY TO REALIZE

THROUGH SHAPE COLOR AND SIZE

DESPITE DIFFERENCE AND VARIETY

LOVE ALONE

CAN RADIATE PEACE IN SOCIETY

LOVE ALONE

CAN TRANSFORM THE ANXIETY

THAT CHOOSES TO WASTE

RATHER THAN EMBRACE

THE LIFELONG REVOLUTION

OF REPETITION

WHICH LIKE A MAGICIAN

THROUGH ATTRITION

OF ROUGH AND TUMBLE

WATER AND STONE

EXPOSING THE NEVER-ENDING WORK

OF LOVE ALONE

FABRICATING A NEW

UNIVERSAL CONDITION

LIBERATING THE INTUITION

FOR EACH PERSON'S MISSION

IN LIFE AND IN DEATH RENDERING

THE CRUCIBLE BEAUTIFUL

BEAUTY DETECTED

BEAUTY RESPECTED

BEAUTY PROTECTED

BEAUTY COLLECTED

ON YOUR SHORES ONTARIO

LAKE DESIGNATED GREAT

SPEWING FORTH GLASS

CHARGED WITH

INDESCRIBABLE BEAUTY

HERE AND NOW

Palavas, France ~ August 6, 2017

The Transfiguration

HERE AND NOW

FOREVER YET TO COME

IS ETERNITY FOR ALL

OR JUST FOR SOME

IF WE STAND DIVIDED

IT'S BETTER WE FALL

CRAWL IN THE CALL

TO LIVE AS ONE

ENVELOPING COMMUNION

HUMAN REVOLUTION

DIVINE INSTITUTION

RECONSTRUCTING EXCLUSION

TRANSFIGURED

ON THE MOUNTAIN

LOVE SHINING

FREELY FLOWING AS

A FIRE FOUNTAIN

SPARKING DAYS

ENDOWING TIME

WITH FOREVER

photography

All Photos are by Fr. Stan except
page 67 and the Front Cover

PAGE 71 ~ Masaka, Uganda, Africa August 2011

PAGE 79 ~ Lake Ontario, Canada September 2016

Front Cover ~ David Gonzalez